Poems in Spanish

Paul Hoover

For Richard
Chicago 2009

[signature]

Also by Paul Hoover

Poetry

Edge and Fold (Apogee Press, forthcoming 2006)
Winter (Mirror) (Flood Editions, 2002)
Rehearsal in Black (Salt Publications, 2001)
Totem and Shadow: New & Selected Poems (Talisman House, 1999)
Viridian (University of Georgia Press, 1997)
The Novel: A Poem (New Directions, 1990)
Idea (The Figures, 1987)
Nervous Songs (L'Epervier Press, 1986)
Somebody Talks a Lot (The Yellow Press, 1983)
Letter to Einstein Beginning Dear Albert. (The Yellow Press, 1979)

Fiction

Saigon, Illinois (Vintage Contemporaries, 1988)

Essays

Fables of Representation (University of Michigan Press, 2004)

Publications Edited

Postmodern American Poetry (W.W. Norton, 1994)
New American Writing, 1986 to present.

Poems in Spanish

Paul Hoover

OMNIDAWN PUBLISHING
RICHMOND, CALIFORNIA
2005

Cover image by Zach Carter courtesy of the artist.

Book cover and interior design by Ken Keegan.

Offset printed in the United States of America
on archival, acid-free recycled paper
by Thomson-Shore, Inc, Dexter, Michigan.

Cataloging-in-Publication Data appear at the end of the book.

Published by Omnidawn Publishing
Richmond, California
www.omnidawn.com
(800) 792-4957

ISBN-13: 978-1-890650-25-4
ISBN-10: 1-890650-25-0

9 8 7 6 5 4 3 2 1

Acknowledgements

Thanks to editors of the following magazines in which these works appeared:

American Poetry Review (David Bonanno, Stephen Berg, Arthur Vogelsang): "Poem in Spanish," "Corazon," "Intention and Its Thing," "Lisbon Story," "The World as Found," "Driver's Song," and the essay "Reality and Its Antecedents"

26 (Avery E.D. Burns, Rusty Morrison, Joseph Noble, Elizabeth Robinson, Brian Strang): "Apology for the Finding"

Volt (Gillian Conoley and Calvin Bedient): "The Mill"

Small Town (Ryan Logan Smith): "Buenos Aires"

Denver Quarterly (Bin Ramke): "Suite for Toy Piano"

Van Gogh's Ear, Paris: "Monster"

New Messes (Ara Shirinyan): "Nature in Black and White," "Poetics," and "Notes at Ground Level"

In the Footsteps of a Shadow: American Poetic Responses to Fernando Pessoa (Charles Cutler): "Lisbon Story"

Jacket (John Tranter): "But Kenneth"

Mi Poesias (Gabriel Gudding): "The Stone" and "The Road"

Contents

I. Poems In Spanish

Poem in Spanish

I have two coffins but only one wife,
who loves me like a neighbor.
I have one wing and a long flight scheduled.

I have two sons and the time of day,
its late hour dark in a brilliant landscape.

I have a small religion based on silence
and a furious heart beating. I have a map
of the region where the kiss is deepest,
a duplex cathedral for my hells and heavens,
and one oily feather.   No matter how I settle,
the world keeps moving at its famous pace.

I have two minds and an eye for seeing
the world's singular problems as my self-portrait.
I have fuzzy lightning and a pair of old glasses.

I have two radios but only one message,
subtle in transmission, arriving like wine.
I have *yo tengo* and two *tambiens*.
The world between them creaks
like distance and difference.

I have two fires and a very sleepy fireman,
immortal longings and one life only,
unliving and undying.

Corazon

Simple things like bread,
you can't even think about them.

The lesson of skin touching skin,
the lesson of earth as it rolls in darkness,
the lesson of things as they are.

The mind collapses under the weight
of so much thinking. It's almost tragic.

The road has no thought of distance.
The road is just the road.

Words don't think us,
words on a table among the other meats,
words like summers passing.

In blue organdy dresses,
the policemen are euphoric.

Transparent and irreverent,
the wide face of lightning
is pressed to water's surface.

The century is thick with history
and the worst of intentions.

The very worst intentions,
and all I can drink lately
is the filthy holy water.

The World as Found

All these things the creator told me in Alabama.
                            —Sun Ra

Mariposa, what a clean word is that!
It can fly around all day
and never get mud on its wings.
It makes a clean sound as it passes right through me—
almost nothing really.

Mud sprawls on the ground, completely helpless.
Who can ever respect it?

Mariposa, butterfly—
so pretty and maybe crazy,
like Blanche Dubois as a girl.
Even *Schmetterling*
has a cadence true to its ideal.

Words in my mouth
are preparing for summer,
giving birth to themselves again.

It isn't rocket science.
Everyone knows their names:
barranco and embankment,
noises and *ruidos*—
get down on your knees and pray!
A beautiful woman is passing,
and, if you insist, a man.
Words of skin and bone.

Where's my *refuge* and my *trap,*
Where do they go when I think them?

All day the words are at me,
coming and going and meaning,
and in the evening also.
It's the traffic of the world.

But at night, if it happens
that I sink into her body,
there is no word, not even *silk*,
to tell you what I'm thinking.
Sound spills from my mouth,
shapeless all around us.

Driver's Song

I shall never reach Danville, Ohio,
Danville distant and lonely.

Black car, small moon,
in the back seat beer.
Because I've forgotten the roads
I shall never reach Danville, Ohio.

Over the plains, through Indiana,
where I was lonely also.
Black car, yellow moon.
My dead father keeps watch over me
from an upstairs window.

What a long way from California
and in what a fast car—
invisible to the soul.

Ahead I see death moving slowly on the road.
I know I will touch her clothing
before I ever reach Danville, Ohio.

Danville, distant and lonely.

The Mill

This is the evening when a bird nests in a hat
left in the street by a flying man, a man of worlds and heat,
of vellum and fog and sculptures that lurk
when we're not looking, this is the evening.

This is the moment when traffic passes as I have taught it to pass,
as I have learned the way, this is the moment.

This is the place where snow was invented.
This is the town it falls on, consisting of three houses
with plastic lights in the doorway, a man who touches his woman
as she likes to be touched—no matter how warm, always snow—
and the hand that turns the world, this is the place.

This is the life that keeps me awake at night,
its distances and skin, and this is time with its foot in a crack,
unable to move yet passing, this is the life.

This is the hour when the crime was committed;
this is the first cause watching. This is the river drowning
and a filthy shadow washing its hands, this is the hour.

This is the little fish eating the big one. This is the man
who lives by the railroad tracks; this is the train passing.

This is the mill where grain was turned, this is the grain
unfinished, and this is the empty bed of the stream
that used to turn the wheel, this is the mill of absence.

The Stone

I find a stone at the beach
that oddly resembles a man,
cut as it was cut,
smoothed as it is smooth.

Accidental man, its cheeks drawn back,
layered cracks where a brain might be.
It looks like a cartoon figure
committing an act of speech.
But there is only the sound of stone
and history having its way.

I show it my own profile,
and it returns the favor.
Its expression rarely changes.

This dark and handsome stone
now sits on my mantelpiece.

It has my own sense of humor,
a modicum of wisdom.
It stares for days at a lottery ticket
I forgot to take to the store.

It gazes at the ceiling,
and wonders about the world.

It's making plans for money, power,
and something a bit like sex.

The stone regards me
when I'm not looking.
We regard each other.

But I'm sure it's only stone,
with gashes for an eye,
a fierce mouth where something cleft it.

I know it doesn't regard me
with anything like attention—
attention finer than gold.
It's human in shape only.
Its eye is empty and empty again.

But it's my stone now.
It lives as a stone lives,
with the comforts of a man.

The Road

My father endures me.
With his soft fists and fat bible,
he beats me and beats me.
He throws the sheep in my direction,
all thistles and thorns,
and yet every evening
I must wash his feet in the flood.

Only death could take him,
with its hands the size of a child,
only death with its style.

Now he sleeps in sweetness.
He disappears and reappears
like the cat you never see.

How often I see him
at the back of some cafe,
a minor god in black sunglasses,
eating his spaghetti—
strands of it on his shoulders
and also in his hair.

Nothing is for certain,
even the uncertain.

And my mother is always passing,
with her taste of other tastes—
of paper, bees, and sharpness.
Something in her is so solid,
so easy to hold in the mind.
But I can feel it breaking.

I wait and wait, with only speed to keep me,
on roads that curve into whiteness.
My parents walk as fast as they can,
their shadows flying behind them,
but keep getting farther away.

There is solitude in the halls of a palace,
where tourists carry their faces.
There is solitude in reason.
But on the green field, everything is present.
All kinds of speech, just beneath the ear!

The Presence

We know it and we feel it—
the fierce will of things

to set themselves apart,
isolated by their beauty,

bereft in isolation.
Museum of the Thing:

the living glove, earthen shoe,
a parakeet's soft feather

that seems to be made of fur—
yellow tuft of sunlight

falling through the air
like nothing but itself,

as water is nothing but water,
grinding and turning as if

there were no passage.
Where does the work get done

that tenders so much beauty
and leaves us in such grief?

Sweetmeat and papaya,
your own face in chrome

with its hint of speed—
all these chaste subjects

love us in their way—
needle & thimble, dog & bone.

Whatever is absent in them,
let it speak its name:

fingerprint, blue smudge,
a typewriter with new keys—

one for infinity and one for sleeping.
Each night the objects come

to watch us in our beds,
above which hang

the dusty family portraits
retreating toward a quaintness

that can only be remembered—
mother in her kingdom

of white gloves and black bibles,
the mouse she trapped in her hand

as it leaped from a cabinet.
And father, poor father,

whose kindness went on forever,
into a clear confusion,

what were those sounds I heard
from the bed beyond the wall?

Which way should I drive now
to find the house we lived in,

vanished including its trees?
Gone the upstairs bedrooms

with their perfect shining floors,
not even a ghost to warm them.

All things come to witness
these absences like objects—

pears so near to ripeness
they melt in the hand

and roads that will only go south,
with a sound of tires like rain.

I Take Away My Head

I take away my hand, which writes and speaks much.
—Jaime Sabines

I take away my mouth,
Which remembers nothing I say,
Though I speak loudly and often,
With everything on my mind.

I take away my heart,
Which never quite forgives me,
And I remove my ears,
Which have no feeling for song.

Moving between two lights,
Over white stones at midnight,
Past nine black boundaries,
I take away my shadow.

Here is history with its burning questions
And theory with its doubt—
I give them to a ridiculous man
Who smells of the sea and slow dancing.

How good it must be for the rain
To roll around on the street
And commingle with each surface.

The world is nothing much—
Grass and rubble and such.
I'll put it into a camera
Filled with silver and potential.

Childhood and Its Double

Everything's more real, once it finds its mirror.
The gray lake and its gray sky,

skin and the sound of drums,
and the back end of a costume horse

confused against the skyline.
Absence turns the corner

and looks into its eyes,
and presence, whatever it was,

has fewer shapes to inhabit.
My grandfather fell asleep

with one leg in the fire,
and now the other one's missing

because its grave is missing.
This is no fiction. Your body changes

seven times, seven times disguised
by the weakest flesh and the strongest,

and then it finds its absence
as a mouth finds language.

Intention and Its Thing

My father stands in a wheat field
with his back to me. He's intent on distance
and the sounds of early evening.
If he turns slightly, I step to keep him faceless.
I like to watch him watching the high clouds pass
in the shapes of cars he's driven.

The wheat is green. It's early in the summer.
How can I show you this furious wheat
whipping at its shadows, pressing hollow into swale
then regaining its composure entirely?

His back is too large for the shirt he's wearing,
and the shirt is too blue—from a discount bin,
the kind that slips from its hanger.

It's a secret place somewhere in Ohio
that was once mistaken for Spain.
The fields are so flat you have to stand on tiptoe.
That's all that I can tell you.

This is what intrigues me—twice I take his picture,
once with the camera, once with my eye.
It's the eye that remembers.

He passes into image, into memory.
Now he can die and be happy, his eyes full,
the camera full, only the landscape anxious.

Mi Hijo

There is no
single poem,

no presence,
no sentence,

no way of
making strange.

All is familiar
in time and

its sequel.
The stand-up

comic knocks
on an old

drone's door.
Poured before

the lord,
darkness at

its source
creates all things,

but here is a tree,
its real world

impeded by
the story it tells.

Señoras y
Señoras,

the caller
might cry,

Ignorance
lives forever

and the soul
dies early,

with a song
on its lips

and celebrity
madness. But

the poor snail
goes along its

silver trail,
well on its

way to what
it already has.

As the leaf
turns neatly

in the wind
it must possess,

a man sees himself
approaching from

a doorway.
My son, he says

blankly to the
wall nearby.

Don't Kill Yourself

Don't kill yourself, Paul.
The world is angry for only a moment
and then it loves you again.
Even its perfect indifference
is love and no love in equal doses.

Don't contemplate some ending
strapped to the hood of a car.
Don't swallow too many donuts.

Stop weeping like an ostrich
and stalking the boundary fences.
Stop batting your eyelashes.

Everyone knows you lost a big one.
Forget about it, my boy.
Everyone loses the big one.
Who do you think you are?

Your life could be a painting,
The Triumph of Inertia.
The shadows flow in the wrong direction,
but the sun is in its sky.

Don't kill yourself with the shovel
we'll have to bury you with.
Don't even look at that gun.

Your babies are still growing.
Don't disappoint them
with the last cliché of your life.

Go play in the sea with your clothes on
or with no clothes, if you wish.

There are plenty of secrets left
to share with perfect strangers.
So live bravely and die exhausted,
both hands in the till.

It's true we remember little
of what you said or did,
but this will improve with time.

Old wine is the best.
The needle will find its thread.

Lisbon Story

Be quiet—a shadow is singing.
A shadow on a yellow wall
is singing about time,
and a man like time is leaning
against a blue wall.
But it's a shadow singing
her heart out in the night.

Beyond this room in the world,
the sounds of the world are passing.
All lives, all cities, are full of sound.
A woman sings of them.
The river and her song
are cutting into the world.

A shadow is moving its mouth . . .
lyric to distraction, a lyric separation
of world and time, thought and mind.
Shadow on the wall—yellow—
where the blue man listens.

This house on the street, dark.
This slant street in the city, small as streets are small.
A sound of birds flying and a sound of paper.
A sound of sharpening knives, quick,
and dogs lifting their legs, thick,
and the girl who drops her doll.

The blue man listens to the world making itself—
a shoe making distance, click,
and snow barely surviving
on the ground it has chosen, gone.
A world as shadow is passing.

But in the yellow room,
a handsome woman is singing, ending,
and the room and its sounds are dark.

Circumference

The second solitude is that of signs.
                                        —di Chirico

The lake is very quiet—serene, one would say—
when seen at a distance beyond the poplar trees,
which speak much but have little to say.
One senses beneath the lake's surface
something undisclosed—a hint or thread
of the world before the flood:
the perfect, the unbroken, the vacancy
on the corner and the vacancies in men.

On closer inspection, with our feet in the mud
of the bank, the lake takes on a troubled life
that might have been our own.
One agitated wave thrusts against another,
smothering it completely—no help for the pain
of the world, for which we have no name.

Like an eccentric wheel, everything goes round a center.
It wobbles and it troubles, but everything goes.
With its force alone, the rain closes windows.
It shoulders toward the gutters, inwardly and alone.

The first solitude is time, and the second is signs.
The third solitude is distance, and the fourth its symptom.
The fifth is the future, which never quite arrives.

The sixth solitude is a mirror; the seventh a crow—
so many solitudes they crowd against the door.

Each night the soft machine stirs in its bed
and the television glows. Everything's at attention
and also at detachment, if we understand the word.
It's like the lake we've mentioned, an unstable material
that stands with indifference but meets with our nerves.

Such were our discussions—revisionary men,
quick to take offense, slow to change the world.

Apology for the Finding

Green might sway
beyond its own going,
might say its own construction

in the toning of a note,
might find its own light,
"susceptible of proof,"

in the quiet of the stream,
might seek the unsaid
in a tautological boat,

might see beyond myth
or myth's speech eaten
by necessity and its mother.

Grendel's dam in the stream
might see in water
her own broad shape

as the real world's bride,
lapidary product
of a winsome mind

green might be hiding
in the process of what?
A silence unnamed

is not unsaid,
green being pleasure
soon to be unheard,

and Beowulf is coming
into circumspection.
How fragile the solid

undivided world,
requiring a life
yet not desiring one.

Here at the spirit's
lunatic fringe,
a primitive semantic

of wind and stone
grips the world
soundly: honeyed eye,

branches snapped,
leather sound of water
pushing through its holes.

Something like change
clasps us to the real.
I have seen rain

and I have seen buildings
adhere to language.
Flesh is description

from structure to the pore.
Anything can be
the map of its presence—

suspensions of belief
require no alibi.
But even in our living

the whole note rings
a series of inventions
that seems like existence

and not a pretty lie.
I am not I
until in darkness

light strikes water
and the whole boat rides.
Each thing begins

in the middle of things,
from which it sets
all things in order,

but each new wrench
and each new waning
disturbs the one control.

Buenos Aires

They have electricity in the church.
                    —Apollinaire

Shall I fly open wide,
at last relent a heaven?
Pardon submission
            & lower still
adore what's made in pain?
I purchase double far
all good my god can hold.

This new face,
its borrowed eye beheld.

The ways of God are men.

Ever clear in outward calm,
            the first once warned.
The eye disfigured is all unseen.
Delicious, green, grotesque and wild,
rank shade & evening sun.

Savage and pensive,
they slack delay and course.
Slow brake the sheer within.
Light hunger for the wolf.

This perverts abuse.
The views in narrow heaven
are through the garden-mould.
            The rapid
earth's river will not tell how.

On the hour's hot field,
the mirror is fringed
with cold names leaning.
          Universal flowers
mantle that thorn.

Eden on the aisle
is a whole day's rock.
          Old living creatures.
Yielded grace. But not
beneath wanton.

The delay that drove him
like an undergrowth east.
          Sheer within the light,
hunger's prey o'erleaped the feast.

Hirelings will climb, restive
and slow. But fear no assault
from these thin brakes. The random
access plan eases into folds.

Cormorants in the stream.
          Thick with longing's
skin, our own edge attests
to slipstream and riot.

On horse days, a rogue.
Then the counter-party.
          As long as no men saw,
they toiled to their reward.

I am hopeful in my way.
          How does one know
all the Chinese whispers,
their epithets and figures?

The primary one and secondary sun
fill you from within.
       Look not upon the dark
nor take apart the page—

it's *this which* rigged
to the grammar of the town.

Suite for Toy Piano

1

leaf stroke from shoulder
to rib, glow and one hard edge
yellow wing on tongue

mouth on mouth, the sensual
and the fact black in mirrors

2

spare lucidity
of each blue lake reclines like
a knife: all is here

the mission of touch, the press
and scatter, lapidary

3

the gears of fortune
darkly turn in leaves and rain;
enter the world's frame

the earth's slow turn is patient
as a kingdom, old as words

4

in a line of ants
rehearsal and logic of
jostled lexicons

under the skin of a verb
leaning toward time and patience

5

bleeding rhymes and names
the lost hours in a trance and
slow burn of crystal

the heaviest spirit plays
I'm old-fashioned, moan's notice

6

beyond the edgeless
nest of story and what it
sheds, periphery's

music's incognito, its
taste of arrival nameless

7

a truth wholly known
tries to remember the stain
of complication—

a toy piano plays
at Double Happiness Bar

8

some kiss may cloud my
memory some arms may hold
a thrill but (uh-uh)

do nothing till you hear it
from me and you never will

9

between posts of meaning,
light's architecture, the real
is momentary

a fragment of speech requests
a burnt match and a slow dance

10
dark window onto
snow and stars, a telephone—
your voice locks the world

into desire, a frankness
and a blessing, meaning's skin

With Sharon Darrow

Monster

While the
rain speaks

volumes, the
lord of

secret doctrines
makes a

monster with
his hands.

Progeny of
the dead,

the unlucky
ghost speaks

in dreams,
his yellow

eye shining.
He passes

unseen the
townsmen standing

in stark
white shirts.

Untermensch
and radiant

shadow in
a well-lighted

world. Sleepless
river, active

camp. *I*
greatly need

a friend.
The creator

touches nature's
secrets, enters

her body
shaking and

profane. With
one convulsive

spark, he
breathes into

matter a
future and

a theory,
sorrow and

a history.
Monster and

man rage
with need

in charnel-
house speeches.

*My person
was hideous*

*and my
stature gigantic.*

Stitched in
flesh, blood

reflections for
the landscape's

eye. Horizons
spread through-

out his
head; the

form of
things dissolves.

Filthy shadows
of brides

abandoned. Rustle
of men

inside their
wives, all

observed by
a restless

mechanism of
mud and

wire. Mockery's
darling. Who

will teach
the greenness

of sun
and willow?

What figure
stands beyond

these palings,
among the

ravings of
summer trees?

Nature in Black and White

In the crossing branches
beneath the leaves,

each letter tangles
secretly its meaning.

Ants on a peony's
slip of sugar

disappear in shadow
but shine in the sun.

Thinking's on its stem,
alert to flatlands

and slow-moving rivers,
outgrowing this place

of sunken signs
and eager tendrils.

All that clamor
notwithstanding,

the eye is a symbol
for all we have married.

A bell wants to ring
inside the ark;

hard things rule
like granite and music.

The blackbird's answer
is never quite

the same, and neither
is the question.

The granular surface
of a bad photograph

composes a nature
of texture and shadow

where the riprap moves
ever so slightly

and lilacs in the dark
might be possessions.

The present is immortal,
the past under construction,

always on the run as
they say of trouble.

As the wind climbs in,
bearing its grit,

the whole world grinds
down to its witness.

Notes at Ground Level

Sunday

Midnight has
no meaning
other than its

hinge. The late
awakening saint
forgives a loss

of nerve but
never of habit.
Continue by

ceasing but creeping
is for getting.
The double

bind of nature
active in defilement
or stinking with

desire enjoys a
game of suchness.
Tathagata's *that*

embraces the
impalement. Idiot
chatter of cups

in kitchens.
As the blah fact
straightens,

wind in its tie,
the silence
pundit speaks

in the breaking
of rivers. Sung
Koo's darlings

as in the
first instance
(dogs sing too).

Monday

Knots in the
method. As
agreement wanes,

moons trouble
waking. You
start making

pictures paintable
as impressions
in the mud

of a bank. Taboo
combinations
of old Norse

masters and modern
wall fractured.
Public executions

or simply
shooting pictures.
Isn't that glass,

taking its
secret out into
the world?

Tuesday

The image is
hidden but language
is a fact every

thing redresses.
Seated in the room
were several

quiet groups
just shy of
apprehension—

invisible yet
attractive. Statues
of rain falling

in Texas or
the wind blowing
south despite

these strictures.
I pressed each
flower along

that street, its
curious odor fading
along with the

garden. As each
sound ripens, experience
of a world

leans in its
saddle and not
the poppy-

cupping. Cecil
Taylor's "relaxed
talons" speak

for the keys.
Straight-laced fanatics
of decomposition

too specific for
the leaves. *AH*
and *EE*. Mountain

at the window.
Angle of repose
and weight's

own thing. An
immense tune
trembles, feels

for its knees
and then
there's breathing.

But Kenneth

For Kenneth Koch

But were these words, like amps and ohms
In heaven? But Industrial Revolutions? But what
Can one say? But nothing. But even realism.

But dew on skin. But resemblance in the parlor.
But this will be our secret and reasons for cement.
But never say hammer to a boy of rose.

But the woman in my shoes, who when
She walks is active, and the men say what?
But the animals' shadows were not as we imagined.

But standing contemplation on its very edge
And chopping down summer even in the cold.
But the "constitution of the inner nation."

But casing the joint for history in ottava rima.
But a feather in its mouth. But Apollo Dionysian
And Zeus remote control. But it is not whatever;

Necessity must live for the silliest Sarajevan:
Tongue muscle, blood fire, all continents
And evenings. But history "lives sideways,"

Which only poetry captures in the sense
Of a sequence. But Kenneth in a portrait
Reading a book for Fairfield Porter, his type-

Writer gleaming, smudges of light around
His eyes and the back of his hand a fiery white
Like the page his mouth is reading. But the curtains

Fluorescent like interiors in Vuillard. But the pale
House at the window suggests another realm though
Not the transcendent. But actual dancing and

Even possible minds. But the metaphysical sweater
Dark at your center from which the viewer's eye,
Tranquil and domestic, can never quite depart.

First on the Run. Then of an Evening

For Marjorie Perloff

My mother has moved the furniture around.
May she become a flourishing living tree,

Aproned young and lovely wanting my baby.
After all, the sky flashes, the great sea yearns.

Ripeness is all; her in her cooling planet—
Rock ledges, laurel fumes, sacred fainting spells.

Just as you feel when you look on the river and sky.
Just like dearest rock bottom.

Out of some subway scuttle, cell or loft,
Old come-all-ye's streel into the streets.

Reconstituting itself in front of you,
Reification won't get you out of the parking lot.

I too felt the curious abrupt questionings stir within me.
I saw the best minds of my generation destroyed by madness.

Everyone suddenly burst out singing.
Empedocles came coughing through the smoke.

Green light envelops everything,
Glazing the pale hair, the duplicate gray standard faces.

Please send for our complete catalogue:
Prayer of pariah, and the lover's cry.

Every poem's got a prosodic lining.
Everything's so far away.

Remember me this summer, under the eaves again,
Released over a city from a highest tower.

Lovely to be like a racehorse,
Light swaying as if clear and torn.

Or set within the iced white hairline
Of a new moon the gibbous rest.

Funny, I thought, that the lights are on this late
Following, leading, leading us where?

Floral commemoratives move across you.
Form is deep in portions your whole life long.

With Maxine Chernoff

Poetics

I have no objectives, no system, no tendency, and no plan.
I have no speech, no tongue, no memory, and no realm.
Because nothing matters, I am consistent, committed, and excited.
I prefer the definite, the bounded, the repressed and the weak.
Not objectivity but neutrality of being.
Not spontaneity but panic.
For only seeing believes and only the body thinks.
For success is common to those who fail.
For the world's beauty is fading because the world is fading.
For the best narrative is always oblique.
For thought only thinks it thinks—all has been foretold.
For without cruelty, there would be no beauty.
For kindness is always a little bit tragic.
For the mind's progress is zig-zag and stabs at every tree.
For the best art makes things disappear.

After Gerhard Richter

II. Reality and Its Antecedents (Essay)

Reality and Its Antecedents:
Fifty Statements on Life and Art

(Agree or Disagree)

1. Nature is weak in narrative.
2. Indeterminacy has been overdetermined.
3. Nothing is worse than a reasonable poem.
4. Surrealism is a form of the metaphysical.
5. The metaphysical is a form of empty space.
6. Empty space is the source of all creation.
7. In postmodern culture, irony is taken on faith.
8. Style is feeling in search of a sentence.
9. The future is unlived. But it can be experienced.
10. The sign of a good writer is how variously he expresses his one idea.
11. "It is only the point of view that creates the object" (Saussure).
12. Nothing is less erotic than a paragraph.
13. The future has a long history.
14. The present is always a little behind the times.
15. To read the world is also to write it.
16. The soul is nothing but knows something.
17. The tenets of postmodern cosmology are:
    A. Since nothing has unity including the object, only the broken is real.
    B. The broken (the fragmentary, the flawed, and the half-made) is therefore ideal.
18. Lyric poetry rescues pain from the jaws of pleasure.
19. "Beauty—impurities in the rock" (Lorine Niedecker).

20. "The poet takes too many messages" (Jack Spicer).

21. A poem creates pleasure through the impossibility of completely grasping it.

22. The folk poet is "one-among-the-people," therefore socially at ease.

23. The postmodern poet is "one-among-strangers," therefore restless.

24. Each poem requires a new language.

25. Imagism is objectification in a moment of feeling.

26. Objectivism is imagism in a moment of syntax.

27. Of the senses, touch is most distant.

28. Of the literary genres, poetry and plays are the most ceremonial. This explains their long association.

29. Poetry values the unknown, the real, the potential, and the silent—everything, that is, which has no value.

30. Poetry always begins with a sounding.

31. Poetry is closer to the rune and spell than it is to conversation.

32. Lyricism is slowness, as in the drawing of a curved line. This is why nature, which has no straight lines (Emerson), is often so sublime.

33. Artifice is also required of the authentic.

34. "Man is a curious being whose center of gravity is not in himself" (Francis Ponge).

35. "The eye has knowledge the mind cannot share" (Hayden Carruth).

36. Poetry is desire having words with itself.

37. The unstitching of a line (Yeats) is more important than its stitching.

38. Life is closer to art than it is to aesthetics.

39. Nothingness is only a concept—the world is filled.

40. The symbol for infinity should be on the keyboard.

41. The most impressive thing about a parade is the leisure you have to watch it.

42. The tragic hero is a bad reader.

43. Irony is a form of sincerity.

44. Music is silence making itself complex.

45. "All deep things are song" (Thomas Carlyle).

46. The closer it is to absurdity (without passing into it), the better a work of art.

47. Without thought, there can be no feeling.

48. Poetry might as well be profound.

49. The serenity of objects disguises their anxiety.

50. "If Galileo had said in verse that the world moved, the Inquisition would have left him alone" (Thomas Hardy).

Editor of the influential anthology *Postmodern American Poetry*, co-editor of the literary magazine *New American Writing*, and author of nine previous poetry collections, Paul Hoover is Visiting Professor of Creative Writing at San Francisco State University. *Fables of Representation*, his collection of literary essays, was published in 2004. His prizes include the Jerome J. Shestack Award from *American Poetry Review*, an NEA Fellowship in poetry, and the GE Foundation Award for Younger Writers. With Maxine Chernoff, he has translated the selected poetry of Friedrich Hölderlin and, with Nguyen Do, the work of seventeen contemporary Vietnamese poets.

green press
INITIATIVE

Omnidawn Publishing is committed to preserving ancient forests and natural resources. We elected to print *Poems In Spanish* on 50% post consumer recycled paper, processed chlorine free. As a result, for this printing, we have saved:

2 trees (40' tall and 6-8" diameter)
637 gallons of water
256 kilowatt hours of electricity
70 pounds of solid waste
138 pounds of greenhouse gases

Omnidawn Publishing made this paper choice because our printer, Thomson-Shore, Inc., is a member of Green Press Initiative, a nonprofit program dedicated to supporting authors, publishers, and suppliers in their efforts to reduce their use of fiber obtained from endangered forests.

For more information, visit www.greenpressinitiative.org

Library of Congress Cataloging-in-Publication Data

Hoover, Paul, 1946-
    Poems in Spanish / by Paul Hoover.
        p. cm.
    ISBN-13: 978-1-890650-25-4 (acid-free paper)
    ISBN-10: 1-890650-25-0 (acid-free paper)
    I. Title.
    PS3558.O6335P64 2005
    811'.54--dc22
                        2005014886